CHRISTMAS SONGS _for_
EASY CLASSICAL GUITAR

Arranged by Mark Phillips

ISBN 978-1-4803-9299-1

7777 W. BLUEMOUND RD. P.O. BOX 13819 MILWAUKEE, WI 53213

Visit Hal Leonard Online at
www.halleonard.com

CONTENTS

Caroling, Caroling

Words by Wihla Hutson
Music by Alfred Burt

Christmas Time Is Here

from A CHARLIE BROWN CHRISTMAS

Words by Lee Mendelson
Music by Vince Guaraldi

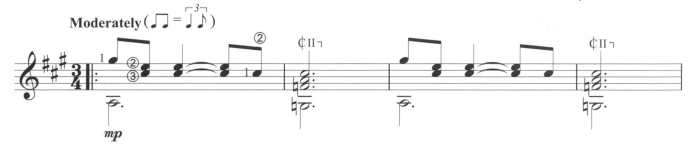

The Christmas Song
(Chestnuts Roasting on an Open Fire)

Music and Lyric by Mel Torme and Robert Wells

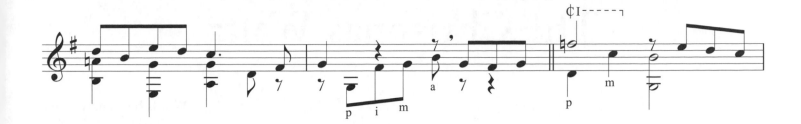

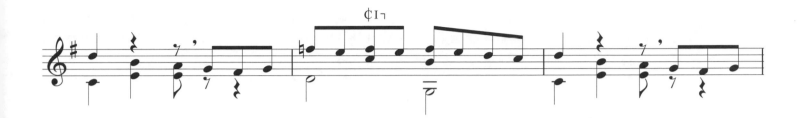

The Christmas Waltz

Words by Sammy Cahn
Music by Jule Styne

Do You Hear What I Hear

Words and Music by Noel Regney and Gloria Shayne

Frosty the Snow Man

Words and Music by Steve Nelson and Jack Rollins

Drop D tuning:
(low to high) D-A-D-G-B-E

Moderately, in 2

Happy Holiday

from the Motion Picture Irving Berlin's HOLIDAY INN

Words and Music by Irving Berlin

Have Yourself a Merry Little Christmas

from MEET ME IN ST. LOUIS

Words and Music by Hugh Martin and Ralph Blane

Moderately slow

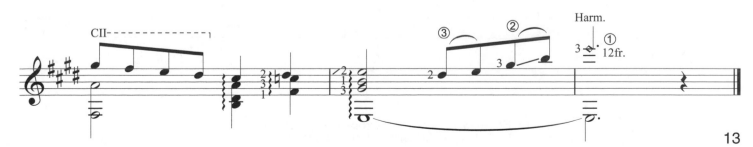

Here Comes Santa Claus
(Right Down Santa Claus Lane)

Words and Music by Gene Autry and Oakley Haldeman

(There's No Place Like)
Home for the Holidays

Words and Music by Al Stillman and Robert Allen

I Wonder as I Wander

By John Jacob Niles

I'll Be Home for Christmas

Words and Music by Kim Gannon and Walter Kent

Let It Snow! Let It Snow! Let It Snow!

Words by Sammy Cahn
Music by Jule Styne

Merry Christmas, Darling

Words and Music by Richard Carpenter and Frank Pooler

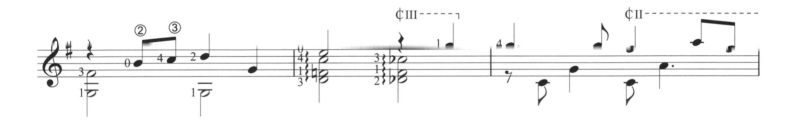

rit.

The Most Wonderful Day of the Year

Music and Lyrics by Johnny Marks

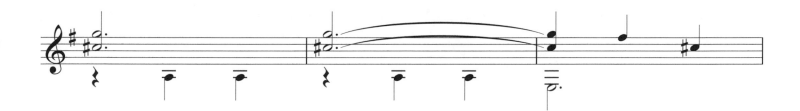

D.S. al Coda
(no repeat)

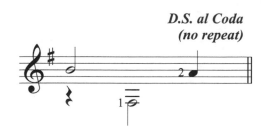

⊕ Coda

23

The Most Wonderful Time of the Year

Words and Music by Eddie Pola and George Wyle

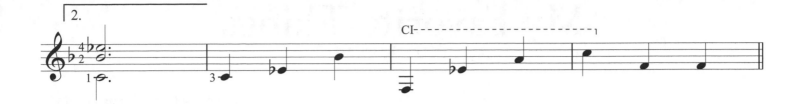

D.S. al Coda
(no repeat)

Coda

My Favorite Things

from THE SOUND OF MUSIC

Lyrics by Oscar Hammerstein II
Music by Richard Rodgers

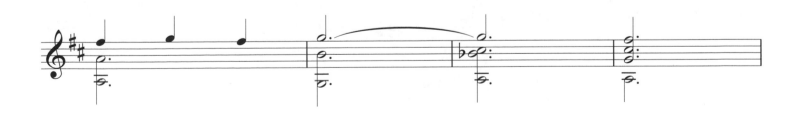

Santa Claus Is Comin' to Town

Words by Haven Gillespie
Music by J. Fred Coots

Silver and Gold

Music and Lyrics by Johnny Marks

Silver Bells

from the Paramount Picture THE LEMON DROP KID

Words and Music by Jay Livingston and Ray Evans

Somewhere in My Memory

from the Twentieth Century Fox Motion Picture HOME ALONE

Words by Leslie Bricusse
Music by John Williams

Moderately

Sleigh Ride

Music by Leroy Anderson

D.S. al Coda
(take repeat)

Coda

D.S. al Fine
(take repeat)

The Star Carol

Lyric by Wihla Hutson
Music by Alfred Burt

Moderately

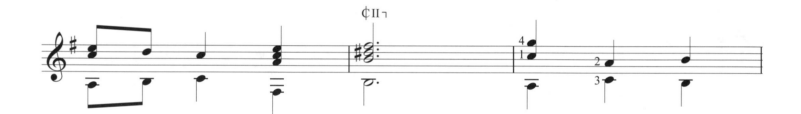

White Christmas

from the Motion Picture Irving Berlin's HOLIDAY INN

Words and Music by Irving Berlin

Slowly, in 2

Winter Wonderland

Words by Dick Smith
Music by Felix Bernard

CELEBRATE CHRISTMAS
WITH YOUR GUITAR AND HAL LEONARD

THE BEST CHRISTMAS GUITAR FAKE BOOK EVER – 2ND EDITION

INCLUDES TAB

Over 150 Christmas classics for guitar. Songs include: Blue Christmas • The Chipmunk Song • Frosty the Snow Man • Happy Holiday • A Holly Jolly Christmas • I Saw Mommy Kissing Santa Claus • I Wonder As I Wander • Jingle-Bell Rock • Rudolph, the Red-Nosed Reindeer • Santa Bring My Baby Back (To Me) • Suzy Snowflake • Tennessee Christmas • and more.
00240053 Melody/Lyrics/Chords $19.95

THE BIG CHRISTMAS COLLECTION FOR EASY GUITAR

Includes over 70 Christmas favorites, such as: Ave Maria • Blue Christmas • Deck the Hall • Feliz Navidad • Frosty the Snow Man • Happy Holiday • A Holly Jolly Christmas • Joy to the World • O Holy Night • Silver and Gold • Suzy Snowflake • and more. Does not include TAB.
00698978 Easy Guitar $16.95

CHRISTMAS

INCLUDES TAB

Guitar Play-Along Volume 22
Book/CD Pack

8 songs: The Christmas Song (Chestnuts Roasting on an Open Fire) • Frosty the Snow Man • Happy Xmas (War Is Over) • Here Comes Santa Claus (Right Down Santa Claus Lane) • Jingle-Bell Rock • Merry Christmas, Darling • Rudolph the Red-Nosed Reindeer • Silver Bells.
00699600 Guitar Tab $15.95

CHRISTMAS CAROLS

Guitar Chord Songbook

80 favorite carols for guitarists who just need the lyrics and chords: Angels We Have Heard on High • Away in a Manger • Deck the Hall • Good King Wenceslas • The Holly and the Ivy • Irish Carol • Jingle Bells • Joy to the World • O Holy Night • Rocking • Silent Night • Up on the Housetop • Welsh Carol • What Child Is This? • and more.
00699536 Lyrics/Chord Symbols/Guitar Chord Diagrams $12.99

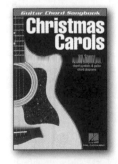

CHRISTMAS CAROLS

INCLUDES TAB

Guitar Play-Along Volume 62
Book/CD Pack

8 songs: God Rest Ye Merry, Gentlemen • Hark! The Herald Angels Sing • It Came upon the Midnight Clear • O Come, All Ye Faithful (Adeste Fideles) • O Holy Night • Silent Night • We Three Kings of Orient Are • What Child Is This?
00699798 Guitar Tab $12.95

CHRISTMAS CAROLS

INCLUDES TAB

Jazz Guitar Chord Melody Solos

Chord melody arrangements in notes & tab of 26 songs of the season. Includes: Auld Lang Syne • Deck the Hall • Good King Wenceslas • Here We Come A-Wassailing • Joy to the World • O Little Town of Bethlehem • Toyland • We Three Kings of Orient Are • and more.
00701697 Solo Guitar $12.99

THE CHRISTMAS GUITAR COLLECTION

INCLUDES TAB

Book/CD Pack

20 beautiful fingerstyle arrangements of contemporary Christmas favorites, including: Blue Christmas • Feliz Navidad • Happy Xmas (War Is Over) • I Saw Mommy Kissing Santa Claus • I'll Be Home for Christmas • A Marshmallow World • The Most Wonderful Time of the Year • What Are You Doing New Year's Eve? • and more. CD includes full demos of each piece.
00700181 Fingerstyle Guitar $17.95

CLASSICAL GUITAR CHRISTMAS COLLECTION

INCLUDES TAB

Includes classical guitar arrangements in standard notation and tablature for more than two dozen beloved carols: Angels We Have Heard on High • Auld Lang Syne • Ave Maria • Away in a Manger • Canon in D • The First Noel • I Saw Three Ships • Joy to the World • O Christmas Tree • O Holy Night • Silent Night • What Child Is This? • and more.
00699493 Guitar Solo $9.95

FINGERPICKING CHRISTMAS

INCLUDES TAB

Features 20 classic carols for the intermediate-level guitarist. Includes: Away in a Manger • Deck the Hall • The First Noel • It Came upon the Midnight Clear • Jingle Bells • O Come, All Ye Faithful • Silent Night • We Wish You a Merry Christmas • What Child Is This? • and more.
00699599 Solo Guitar $8.95

FINGERPICKING CHRISTMAS CLASSICS

INCLUDES TAB

15 favorite holiday tunes, with each solo combining melody and harmony in one superb fingerpicking arrangement. Includes: Christmas Time Is Here • Feliz Navidad • I Saw Mommy Kissing Santa Claus • Mistletoe and Holly • My Favorite Things • Santa Baby • Somewhere in My Memory • and more.
00701695 Solo Guitar $7.99

FINGERPICKING YULETIDE

INCLUDES TAB

Carefully written for intermediate-level guitarists, this collection includes an introduction to fingerstyle guitar and 16 holiday favorites: Do You Hear What I Hear • Happy Xmas (War Is Over) • A Holly Jolly Christmas • Jingle-Bell Rock • Rudolph the Red-Nosed Reindeer • and more.
00699654 Fingerstyle Guitar $9.99

THE ULTIMATE CHRISTMAS GUITAR SONGBOOK

100 songs in a variety of notation styles, from easy guitar and classical guitar arrangements to note-for-note guitar tab transcriptions. Includes: All Through the Night • Auld Lang Syne • Away in a Manger • Blue Christmas • The Chipmunk Song • The Gift • I've Got My Love to Keep Me Warm • Jingle Bells • One Bright Star • Santa Baby • Silver Bells • Wonderful Christmastime • and more.
00700185 Multi-Arrangements $19.95

0414

CLASSICAL GUITAR

PUBLICATIONS FROM HAL LEONARD

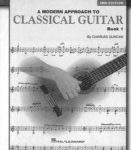

THE BEATLES FOR CLASSICAL GUITAR

Includes 20 solos from big Beatles hits arranged for classical guitar, complete with left-hand and right-hand fingering. Songs include: All My Loving • And I Love Her • Can't Buy Me Love • Fool on the Hill • From a Window • Hey Jude • If I Fell • Let It Be • Michelle • Norwegian Wood • Obla Di • Ticket to Ride • Yesterday • and more. Features arrangements and an introduction by Joe Washington, as well as his helpful hints on classical technique and detailed notes on how to play each song. The book also covers parts and specifications of the classical guitar, tuning, and Joe's "Strata System" – an easy-reading system applied to chord diagrams.

_____ 00699237 Classical Guitar.....................$19.99

CZERNY FOR GUITAR
12 SCALE STUDIES FOR CLASSICAL GUITAR
by David Patterson

Adapted from Carl Czerny's *School of Velocity, Op. 299* for piano, this lesson book explores 12 keys with 12 different approaches or "treatments." You will explore a variety of articulations, ranges and technical perspectives as you learn each key. These arrangements will not only improve your ability to play scales fluently, but will also develop your ears, knowledge of the fingerboard, reading abilities, strength and endurance. In standard notation and tablature.

_____ 00701248 ....$9.99

MATTEO CARCASSI – 25 MELODIC AND PROGRESSIVE STUDIES, OP. 60
arr. Paul Henry

One of Carcassi's (1792-1853) most famous collections of classical guitar music – indispensable for the modern guitarist's musical and technical development. Performed by Paul Henry. 49-minute audio accompaniment.

_____ 00696506 Book/CD Pack......................$17.95

CLASSICAL & FINGERSTYLE GUITAR TECHNIQUES
by David Oakes • Musicians Institute

This Master Class with MI instructor David Oakes is aimed at any electric or acoustic guitarist who wants a quick, thorough grounding in the essentials of classical and fingerstyle technique. Topics covered include: arpeggios and scales, free stroke and rest stroke, P-i scale technique, three-to-a-string patterns, natural and artificial harmonics, tremolo and rasgueado, and more. The book includes 12 intensive lessons for right and left hand in standard notation & tab, and the CD features 92 solo acoustic tracks.

_____ 00695171 Book/CD Pack......................$17.99

CLASSICAL GUITAR CHRISTMAS COLLECTION

Includes classical guitar arrangements in standard notation and tablature for more than two dozen beloved carols: Angels We Have Heard on High • Auld Lang Syne • Ave Maria • Away in a Manger • Canon in D • The First Noel • God Rest Ye Merry, Gentlemen • Hark! the Herald Angels Sing • I Saw Three Ships • Jesu, Joy of Man's Desiring • Joy to the World • O Christmas Tree • O Holy Night • Silent Night • What Child Is This? • and more.

_____ 00699493 Guitar Solo $9.95

CLASSICAL GUITAR WEDDING

Perfect for players hired to perform for someone's big day, this songbook features 16 classsical wedding favorites arranged for solo guitar in standard notation and tablature. Includes: Air on the G String • Ave Maria • Bridal Chorus • Canon in D • Jesu, Joy of Man's Desiring • Minuet • Sheep May Safely Graze • Wedding March • and more.

_____ 00699563 Solo Guitar with Tab..............$10.95

CLASSICAL MASTERPIECES FOR GUITAR

27 works by Bach, Beethoven, Handel, Mendelssohn, Mozart and more transcribed with standard notation and tablature. Now anyone can enjoy classical material regardless of their guitar background. Also features stay-open binding.

_____ 00699312 ....$12.95

MASTERWORKS FOR GUITAR
Over 60 Favorites from Four Centuries
World's Great Classical Music

Dozens of classical masterpieces: Allemande • Bourree • Canon in D • Jesu, Joy of Man's Desiring • Lagrima • Malaguena • Mazurka • Piano Sonata No. 14 in C# Minor (Moonlight) Op. 27 No. 2 First Movement Theme • Ode to Joy • Prelude No. I (Well-Tempered Clavier).

_____ 00699503 ....$16.95

A MODERN APPROACH TO CLASSICAL GUITAR
by Charles Duncan

This multi-volume method was developed to allow students to study the art of classical guitar within a new, more contemporary framework. For private, class or self-instruction. Book One incorporates chord frames and symbols, as well as a recording to assist in tuning and to provide accompaniments for at-home practice. Book One also introduces beginning fingerboard technique and music theory. Book Two and Three build upon the techniques learned in Book One.

_____ 00695114 Book 1 – Book Only...............$6.99
_____ 00695113 Book 1 – Book/CD Pack $10.99
_____ 00695116 Book 2 – Book Only...............$6.99
_____ 00695115 Book 2 – Book/CD Pack $10.99
_____ 00699202 Book 3 – Book Only...............$7.95
_____ 00695117 Book 3 – Book/CD Pack $10.95
_____ 00695119 Composite Book/CD Pack.....$29.99

ANDRES SEGOVIA – 20 STUDIES FOR GUITAR
Sor/Segovia

20 studies for the classical guitar written by Beethoven's contemporary, Fernando Sor, revised, edited and fingered by the great classical guitarist Andres Segovia. These essential repertoire pieces continue to be used by teachers and students to build solid classical technique. Features a 50-minute demonstration CD.

_____ 00695012 Book/CD Pack......................$18.95
_____ 00006363 Book Only $7.99

THE FRANCISCO COLLECTION TÁRREGA
edited and performed by Paul Henry

Considered the father of modern classical guitar, Francisco Tárrega revolutionized guitar technique and composed a wealth of music that will be a cornerstone of classical guitar repertoire for centuries to come. This unique book/CD pack features 14 of his most outstanding pieces in standard notation and tab, edited and performed on CD by virtuoso Paul Henry. Includes: Adelita • Capricho Árabe • Estudio Brillante • Grand Jota • Lágrima • Malagueña • María • Recuerdos de la Alhambra • Tango • and more, plus bios of Tárrega and Henry.

_____ 00698993 Book/CD Pack......................$19.99

HAL•LEONARD CORPORATION

7777 W. BLUEMOUND RD. P.O. BOX 13819 MILWAUKEE, WI 53213

Visit Hal Leonard Online at **www.halleonard.com**

Prices, contents and availability subject to change without notice.

FINGERPICKING GUITAR BOOKS

Hone your fingerpicking skills with these great songbooks featuring solo guitar arrangements in standard notation and tablature. The arrangements in these books are carefully written for intermediate-level guitarists. Each song combines melody and harmony in one superb guitar fingerpicking arrangement. Each book also includes an introduction to basic fingerstyle guitar.

FINGERPICKING ACOUSTIC
00699614.................................$10.99

FINGERPICKING ACOUSTIC ROCK
00699764...................................$9.99

FINGERPICKING BACH
00699793...................................$8.95

FINGERPICKING BALLADS
00699717...................................$9.99

FINGERPICKING BEATLES
00699049.................................$19.99

FINGERPICKING BEETHOVEN
00702390...................................$7.99

FINGERPICKING BLUES
00701277 ....$7.99

FINGERPICKING BROADWAY FAVORITES
00699843...................................$9.99

FINGERPICKING BROADWAY HITS
00699838...................................$7.99

FINGERPICKING CELTIC FOLK
00701148...................................$7.99

FINGERPICKING CHILDREN'S SONGS
00699712...................................$9.99

FINGERPICKING CHRISTIAN
00701076 ....$7.99

FINGERPICKING CHRISTMAS
00699599...................................$8.95

FINGERPICKING CHRISTMAS CLASSICS
00701695...................................$7.99

FINGERPICKING CLASSICAL
00699620...................................$8.95

FINGERPICKING COUNTRY
00699687...................................$9.99

FINGERPICKING DISNEY
00699711.................................$10.99

FINGERPICKING DUKE ELLINGTON
00699845...................................$9.99

FINGERPICKING ENYA
00701161...................................$9.99

FINGERPICKING GOSPEL
00701059...................................$7.99

FINGERPICKING GUITAR BIBLE
00691040 ....$19.99

FINGERPICKING HYMNS
00699688...................................$8.95

FINGERPICKING IRISH SONGS
00701965...................................$7.99

FINGERPICKING JAZZ FAVORITES
00699844 ....$7.99

FINGERPICKING JAZZ STANDARDS
00699840...................................$7.99

FINGERPICKING LATIN FAVORITES
00699842...................................$9.99

FINGERPICKING LATIN STANDARDS
00699837...................................$7.99

FINGERPICKING ANDREW LLOYD WEBBER
00699839...................................$9.99

FINGERPICKING LOVE SONGS
00699841...................................$9.99

FINGERPICKING LOVE STANDARDS
00699836 ....$9.99

FINGERPICKING LULLABYES
00701276...................................$9.99

FINGERPICKING MOVIE MUSIC
00699919...................................$9.99

FINGERPICKING MOZART
00699794...................................$8.95

FINGERPICKING POP
00699615...................................$9.99

FINGERPICKING PRAISE
00699714...................................$8.95

FINGERPICKING ROCK
00699716...................................$9.99

FINGERPICKING STANDARDS
00699613...................................$9.99

FINGERPICKING WEDDING
00699637...................................$9.99

FINGERPICKING WORSHIP
00700554...................................$7.99

**FINGERPICKING NEIL YOUNG –
GREATEST HITS**
00700134.................................$12.99

FINGERPICKING YULETIDE
00699654...................................$9.99

HAL•LEONARD®
CORPORATION
7777 W. BLUEMOUND RD. P.O. BOX 13819 MILWAUKEE, WI 53213

Visit Hal Leonard online at **www.halleonard.com**

Prices, contents and availability subject to change without notice.

0114

THE PUBLICATIONS OF
CHRISTOPHER PARKENING

CHRISTOPHER PARKENING – DUETS AND CONCERTOS

Throughout his career, Christopher Parkening has had the opportunity to perform with many of the world's leading artists and orchestras, and this folio contains many selections from those collaborations. All of the pieces included here have been edited and fingered for the guitar by Christopher Parkening himself.
00690938...$24.99

THE CHRISTOPHER PARKENING GUITAR METHOD, VOL. 1 – REVISED

in collaboration with
Jack Marshall and David Brandon

Learn the art of the classical guitar with this premier method for beginners by one of the world's preeminent virtuosos and the recognized heir to the legacy of Andrés Segovia. Learn basic classical guitar technique by playing beautiful pieces of music, including over 50 classical pieces, 26 exercises, and 14 duets. Includes notes in the first position, how to hold the guitar, tuning, right and left hand technique, arpeggios, tone production, placement of fingers and nails, flats, naturals, key signatures, the bar, and more. Also includes many helpful photos and illustrations, plus sections on the history of the classical guitar, selecting a guitar, guitar care, and more.
00695228 Book..$12.99
00696023 Book/CD Pack..$19.99

THE CHRISTOPHER PARKENING GUITAR METHOD, VOL. 2

Intermediate to Upper-Intermediate Level

Continues where Vol. 1 leaves off. Teaches: all notes in the upper position; tone production; advanced techniques such as tremolo, harmonics, vibrato, pizzicato and slurs; practice tips; stylistic interpretation; and more. The first half of the book deals primarily with technique, while the second half of the book applies the technique with repertoire pieces. As a special bonus, this book includes 32 previously unpublished Parkening edition pieces by composers including Dowland, Bach, Scarlatti, Sor, Tarrega and other, plus three duets for two guitars.
00695229 Book..$12.95
00696024 Book/CD Pack..$19.99

PARKENING AND THE GUITAR – VOL. 1

Music of Two Centuries:
Popular New Transcriptions for Guitar
Virtuoso Music for Guitar

Ten transcriptions for solo guitar of beautiful music from many periods and styles, edited and fingered by Christopher Parkening. All pieces are suitable for performance by the advanced guitarist. Ten selections: Afro-Cuban Lullaby • Empress of the Pagodes (Ravel) • Menuet (Ravel) • Minuet in D (Handel) • Passacaille (Weiss) • Pastourelle (Poulenc) • Pavane for a Dead Princess (Ravel) • Pavane for a Sleeping Beauty (Ravel) • Preambulo (Scarlatti-Ponce) • Sarabande (Handel).
00699105...$9.95

PARKENING AND THE GUITAR – VOL. 2

Music of Two Centuries:
Popular New Transcriptions for Guitar
Virtuoso Music for Guitar

Nine more selections for the advanced guitarist: Clair de Lune (Debussy) • Giga (Visée) • The Girl with the Flaxen Hair (Debussy) • Gymnopedie Nos. I-III (Satie) • The Little Shepherd (Debussy) • The Mysterious Barricades (Couperin) • Sarabande (Debussy).
00699106...$9.95

CHRISTOPHER PARKENING – ROMANZA

Virtuoso Music for Guitar

Three wonderful transcriptions edited and fingered by Parkening: Catalonian Song • Rumores de la Caleta • Romance.
00699103...$7.95

CHRISTOPHER PARKENING – SACRED MUSIC FOR THE GUITAR, VOL. 1

Seven inspirational arrangements, transcriptions and compositions covering traditional Christian melodies from several centuries. These selections appear on the Parkening album Sacred Music for the Guitar. Includes: Präludium (Bach) • Our Great Savior • God of Grace and God of Glory (2 guitars) • Brethren, We Have Met to Worship • Deep River • Jesus, We Want to Meet • Evening Prayer.
00699095...$10.95

CHRISTOPHER PARKENING – SACRED MUSIC FOR THE GUITAR, VOL. 2

Seven more selections from the album *Sacred Music for the Guitar:* Hymn of Christian Joy (guitar and harpsichord) • Simple Gifts • Fairest Lord Jesus • Stir Thy Church, O God Our Father • All Creatures of Our God and King • Glorious Things of Thee Are Spoken • Praise Ye the Lord (2 guitars).
00699100...$10.95

CHRISTOPHER PARKENING – SOLO PIECES

Sixteen transcriptions for solo guitar edited and fingered by Parkening, including: Allegro • Danza • Fugue • Galliard • I Stand at the Threshold • Prelude • Sonata in D • Suite Española • Suite in D Minor • and more.
00690939...$19.99

PARKENING PLAYS BACH

Virtuoso Music for Guitar

Nine transcriptions edited and fingered by Parkening: Preludes I, VI & IX • Gavottes I & II • Jesu, Joy of Man's Desiring • Sheep May Safely Graze • Wachet Auf, Ruft Uns Die Stemme • Be Thou with Me • Sleepers Awake (2 guitars).
00699104...$9.95

CHRISTOPHER PARKENING – VIRTUOSO PERFORMANCES

This DVD features performances and career highlights from classical guitar virtuoso Christopher Parkening (filmed in 1971, 1973, 1998 and 2003). Viewers can watch feature titles in their entirety or select individual songs. As a bonus, there is archival footage of Andrés Segovia performing in studio, circa 1950. The DVD also includes an informational booklet. 95 minutes.
00320506 DVD $24.99

HAL•LEONARD® CORPORATION
7777 W. BLUEMOUND RD. P.O. BOX 13819
MILWAUKEE, WISCONSIN 53213

Prices, contents and availability subject to change without notice.